YORK

TERRY DEARY

Illustrated by Mike Phillips

■SCHOLASTIC

To Bruce Todd of the White Swan in Minskip -
the best pub in Yorkshire.

Scholastic Children's Books,
Euston House, 24 Eversholt Street,
London NW1 1DB, UK
A division of Scholastic Ltd
London ~ New York ~ Toronto ~ Sydney ~ Auckland
Mexico City ~ New Delhi ~ Hong Kong

Published in the UK by Scholastic Ltd, 2005

10 digit ISBN 0 439 95392 8
13 digit ISBN 978 0439 95392 4

Typeset by M Rules
Printed and bound in Denmark by Nørhaven Paperback A/S, Viborg

4 6 8 10 9 7 5 3

CONTENTS

INTRODUCTION

Go to York today and you will feel quite safe ... except you may be trampled by terrible tourists in summer or finished off by floods in winter.[1]

Or worse – swamped by sightseers in any season...

But York hasn't always been such a safe place.

The Ancient Brit Brigantes would bash you if you weren't careful ... then along came the ruthless Romans to rampage all over.

The smashing Saxons had no sooner settled than along came the vicious Vikings to viscerate everyone in sight.

The Normans were even nastier when they arrived.

But peace finally settled on the city and a man with a scythe wandered quietly through the streets.

1 Heavy rains and melting snow made the River Ouse rise seven metres and flood 800 homes in York in 1982. It wasn't the first time. Flood defences were built costing eight million pounds so it wouldn't happen again. In November 2000 it happened again – the worst floods for 400 years. Then again in January 2005. No wonder it's called 'the most regularly flooded city in Britain'.

The Tudors were terrible torturers and the Stuarts tore York's Guy Fawkes to pieces.

The Georgians strung up Dick Turpin to stop him robbing you of your horse, your sheep, your purse or your life.

And the Victorians were simply vicious, with at least one savage school teacher having a cupboard full of kids' corpses.

So forget the cute and the quaint city and listen to tales of the horrible human history ...

YORK TIMELINE

AD 71 Rotten Roman army arrives and sets up a camp so it can bash the British Brigantes tribe. They call it Eboracum because no one had thought of calling it York yet.

410 The Romans go home. Along come the Angles and the Saxons from Germany to settle. They capture York ... King Arthur takes it back - but the legendary lord disappears.

600s Saxon warlord Edwin brings Christianity to the place. By 627 there's a little wooden church on the spot where the cathedral stands today.

700s York's name is now Eoforwic - it is top town in the north. The trouble is that will make it top target when those vicious Vikings arrive...

866 The vicious Vikings are here, led by Ivar the Boneless. He shares out the lands with his brother, King Halfden. They call the place Jorvik – but if you say 'Yorvik' you'll see the city has almost decided what to call itself. Two thousand people live there (about the number who go to see York City play football these days).

867 Saxon King Aella tries to attack the Vikings at York. They capture him and execute him horribly.

927 The Saxons can be as savage as the Vikings. King Aethelstan enters York and flattens the Viking fortress so they can't cause him any more trouble. He shares out the Viking loot among his army. Nice man. He orders his own brother to be drowned at sea. Maybe not so nice.

954 Eric Bloodaxe is the last Viking ruler of York. History books say he is 'driven out' by King Eadred of Wessex. Anyway, he is later murdered on a trip 70 miles north. Yorkshire is now part of England and ruled by kings in the south. Still is.

1016 The English Uhtred pops across from Northumberland to see Viking King Canute at Wighill near York and make peace but he never gets there. He is ambushed by his old enemy Thurbrand. Canute probably set up the slaughter.

1066 King Harold fights a bitter battle near York – Stamford Bridge – and defeats the Viking leader Hardrada. He comes to York to have a party ... then gets the bad news: the Normans have landed on the south coast. Harold will lose that battle.

1069 William the Conqueror has arrived with his Normans and they're here to stay. They build a couple of wooden castles in York but the Saxons massacre the Norman defenders. The Normans take a vicious revenge – they are also here to slay. They rob the churches and the cathedral while they are in an avenging mood. King William spends the winter in York.

1190 The Jewish people are being attacked by the people of York. They flee to the castle but their enemies surround it. The Jews set fire to it and many kill themselves rather than surrender. The ones who surrender are murdered anyway.

1349 Around 13,000 people are living in York until ... along comes the Black Death, the plague that wipes out half the people in the city. Even by the year 1500 there are still only 10,000 in the city.

1400s The wool business is moving to other places. York is losing people and becoming poorer. It's a worry.

1453–1487 The Wars of the Roses don't help the poor people of York. The York family is battling the Lancaster family – but the people of York support the Lancaster side ...

got that? York family King Edward IV gets upset. He rules York harshly.

1472 The new cathedral (York Minster) is finally finished in 1472. It's only taken them 250 years!

1533 King Henry VIII forms the Church of England (with himself as head) and begins closing down the monasteries. Another of York's big businesses – religion – is going to suffer. But York stays England's No. 2 city, though life is made worse by plagues (again) in 1550, 1604, 1631 and 1645.

1603 King James VI makes the Council of the North (posh law courts) a strong force in York. The city is on its way back up.

1644 The English Civil War – Parliament and the Roundhead soldiers against King Charles I and his Cavalier soldiers. The Roundheads surround the city. Prince Rupert fights them outside the city at Marston Moor. He loses and York surrenders.

1719 York is becoming quite a popular place with the posh. The coach to London takes four days but the journey time will be down to 20 hours by the 1830s as the roads get better.

1739 Highwayman Dick Turpin is hanged in York for horse-stealing.

1832 No more plague ... but instead the people of York are struck down by cholera. They turn blue and die. It comes from drinking filthy water and living in crowded slums. It's back in 1849.

1847 For a bit of variety, there's an attack of typhus (a disease spread by lice) in 1847, which kills 403 people.

1839 George Hudson is a ruthless businessman and a bit of a crook. But he brings the railway to York – lots of jobs and new businesses like chocolate factories. How sweet.

1849 Cholera is back.

1870 A really, REALLY cruel new law says there has to be a school for the poor children of York. No, no! Not the POOR children of York – the 'poor' children of York – the ones with no money. Poor children.

BAD BRIT BRIGANTES

The Brigantes people lived in the York area – farming and fighting, shepherding and slaughtering their neighbours. Then the Romans arrived. In AD 51, Queen Cartimandua of the Brigantes had a couple of problems. The first problem was her horrible husband, Venutius. The King didn't like the Romans. He was going to make trouble – there'd be battles and bloodshed. She rather liked the invaders.

Anyway, she was bored with Venutius. He had a gorgeous chariot driver called Vellocatus and she really fancied him.

Her second problem was that the Romans had landed in the south of England and defeated the Brit leader Caractacus. Caractacus had been forced to run away. And where had he run? You guessed it. To Cartimandua.

But what if her Roman friends found out? They'd be upset. They'd probably throw her off the throne. There was only one thing to do ... hand Caractacus over to the Romans. And that's what she did. The rat.

Venutius was furious, of course, and they were separated. She didn't mind that because she was free to marry the lovely Vellocatus. But she DID mind when Venutius attacked her and drove her out of Yorkshire in AD 69.

She turned to her Roman friends for help and in AD 71 they set up a fortress in the heart of Yorkshire – on the spot we now call York.

The Roman writer Tacitus said ...

> *Venutius got the throne – we got the fighting.*

But Tacitus was happy to report his brave Roman lads won in the end...

> *Petillius was the governor of Britain who built a Roman army fortress at York. He at once struck terror into their hearts by attacking the Brigantes. After a series of battles, some quite bloody, Petillius ruled over most of the region.*

We don't know what happened to crafty Cartimandua and her hunky chariot driver – maybe they rode off into the sunset on a chariot made for two.

So that's how York came to be built. All because a British queen had a row with her husband.

VIOLENT VIKINGS

The Vikings came along and called the city Jorvik, which is a bit of a cheek. The nasty Norsemen ruled York (on and off) for about 200 years. They are still remembered today, a thousand years after they left.

What was so horrible about their memory?

Aella – two boneless fellas

In 866 the Viking brothers Ivar the Boneless and Halfden captured York – it wasn't very well defended. Of course, Vikings usually took towns to have a good time robbing and killing, but this time it was personal.

They wanted revenge.

The stories say that Lord Aella of Northumbria had killed their father Ragnar...

THEY DROPPED HIM INTO A PIT FULL OF SNAKES WHO BIT HIM TO DEATH!

HE DIDN'T TASSSTE VERY NICE!

PHT!

So when Aella and his brother attacked York, Ivar and Halfden captured Aella alive. They wanted him to suffer a much nastier death.

15

There is a story that when William the Conqueror attacked the north he found the grave of Ivar the Boneless. He had the corpse dug up because he hated his Viking enemies so much. It was a spiteful and vengeful thing to do.

Did you know...?
Ivar was nicknamed the Boneless. One story says that Ivar had no bones because of a magical curse. Of course anyone without bones would collapse like a jelly.

Did you also know...?
In the 1980s, two historians discovered a male skeleton in a Viking graveyard at Repton, Derbyshire. It was nine feet long – 2.75 metres.

They believed the body was that of Ivar the Boneless.

Head man Uhtred

If you'd gone to York in 1006 you'd have seen the old walls were decorated with heads. They were put there by the warrior chief Uhtred.

Uhtred was fighting for Saxon King Ethelred and set off to defeat the Scots. Not only did he beat them but he beheaded them too.

You can imagine the wives of the Scottish warriors became Scottish worriers...

Uhtred was the head man in the north ... in more ways than one. Then he married Sige of York and made a promise.

Big mistake. Thurbrand was a powerful Viking leader. But Uhtred failed to keep his promise to kill Thurbrand – even bigger mistake.

GOOD TO KNOW WHO YOUR ENEMIES ARE, I'LL REMEMBER

Uhtred went on to marry the daughter of King Ethelred. Her name was Aelfgifu.

I PROMISE TO FIGHT YOUR DAD'S ENEMIES

ESPECIALLY THAT CANUTE

OH, YES. ESPECIALLY CANUTE

In 1016 Viking King Canute invaded England and trusty Uhtred said:

I PROMISED TO FIGHT AELFGIFU'S DAD'S ENEMIES

BIG MISTAKE!

Then King Ethelred died. Aelfgifu's dad, being dead, no longer had any enemies so Uhtred could make peace with Canute. Crafty Canute sent for Uhtred – he told him to come to his camp at Wighill near York. But Canute let Thurbrand know of the plan.

Uhtred agreed to come to Canute's camp. Not only was this the biggest mistake of his life, it was also his last. Thurbrand lay in wait and killed old enemy Uhtred before he got to Canute.

End of story?

No.

The Saxons had this idea called a 'feud' – if you kill a man then that man's family will try to kill you. What happened next?

...and the feud ended. There was no one in Thurbrand's family left alive to carry it on.

Foul Fulford

In 1066 William the Conqueror landed at Hastings and beat the English King Harold. Everyone who has suffered a history lesson has been told that ... though you may have forgotten!

But the FIRST great battle of 1066 was at Fulford on the south edge of York. A Viking invasion smashed the English. If there had been newspapers in 1066 the York headlines would have made rotten reading...

YORK SUN

WEDNESDAY, 20 SEPTEMBER 1066

HOORAY FOR HARDRADA!

This evening the Viking leader Hardrada is top man in Yorkshire. His nice Norwegian army smashed the English Earls at Fulford this afternoon and I was there to see it.

The English held the high ground while Hardrada defended a ditch by the river. The English couldn't be beaten if they stayed up there. But the valiant Viking Hardrada had a perfect plan.

He sent out a weak force to defend the eastern end of the ditch. The English thought they would win easily so they left the hill and attacked. When they were in the ditch Hardrada struck.

The ditch had been damp at the start of the day. Soon it was deep in English blood. The battlefield had been marshy but the Vikings now kept their feet dry – they simply used the English corpses like stepping stones.

Tired but happy Hardrada told me, 'I do not plan to enter the city of York. I do not want it looted. I will take hostages from the city. If the English try to attack again I will massacre the hostages!'

And the victorious Viking means it. I know, I am one of the hostages. York has also delivered 150 children to the Norsemen. So let's welcome our Viking victors.

OUR REPORTER – HAPPY TO GREET HARDRADA!

Hardrada had beaten the northern army, but King Harold arrived with an army from the south and caught the Vikings napping … yes, really!

The Vikings were dozing in the sun at Stamford Bridge – ten miles from Fulford, north-east of York. Harold attacked before most Vikings could get their weapons or armour.

After a bitter battle Harold won. The reporter would have had a different story on that day!

HERO HAROLD HAMMERS HORRIBLE HARDRADA!

The vicious Vikings have been vanquished! And the folk of York say good riddance to the ruthless raiders! Here today, at Stamford Bridge, hopeless Hardrada died with thousands of his awful army when our King's awesome army nobbled the Norse nasties...

There are two famous stories about the battle that everyone in York should know...

1 A lone Viking hero blocked a bridge to stop the English crossing. He gave his friends time to gather some weapons. He killed lots of the English before they killed him with a trick. The English sent a boat under the bridge, pushed a pike through the planks and stabbed him from below.

22

2 Harold offered part of his kingdom to one of the raiders – his brother Tostig. But Tostig wanted land for Hardrada too. Harold answered…

I will give him just seven feet of English land – enough to bury him!

And Harold kept his word. Hardrada died with an arrow in the throat. Tostig was hacked to death when he refused to surrender.

But the battles at Fulford and Stamford Bridge had killed some of England's best warriors. They weren't around to fight William at Hastings a week later so William and his Normans won.

You could say …

THE ENGLISH LOST THE BATTLE OF HASTINGS IN YORK!

DURRR!

NASTY NORMANS

The Normans arrived – and the people of York were not happy to see them. It's as if a stranger moved into your street and said, 'I am your new leader – pay me taxes and do what I say or I'll kill you.' Would YOU welcome them?

A York writer in 1069 said...

The city of York was full of revolt. The people had no respect for the archbishop. Many men lived in tents; they refused to sleep in houses so they should become soft; the Normans called them 'wild men'

Most history books forget about the Vikings once the Normans arrived in 1066. But the Vikings did NOT give up after being beaten at York. They were back in 1069 to try to capture York.

Of course the Normans knew the Vikings would have the help of the English rebels in the city.

THEY HATE US, YOU KNOW! THE VIKINGS, THE ENGLISH, THEY ALL HATE US!

Still, the Normans were safe inside their castle walls.

THEY'RE HIDING IN THEIR HOUSES, WAITING FOR US TO COME OUT. THEY'RE CREEPING CLOSER, I TELL YOU, CREEPING CLOSER!

So what did they do?

WE SET FIRE TO THE CITY

They did a good job of the burning. You could say they did TOO good a job. Setting fire to the houses outside the castle was supposed to give the men in the castle a clear view.

ACTUALLY, WE...ER... DESTROYED A LARGE PART OF THE CITY

Sooner or later the Normans had to leave the castle.

WE RODE OUT TO ATTACK THE ENEMY

What did the Vikings do?

THEY MASSACRED US!

It was a nutty Norman mistake. The remaining Normans tried to escape through a gate in the castle. Waltheof, the Earl of Northumberland, was waiting for them with his long axe. He was said to have chopped 100 Normans. Can you believe that? A Norman gets to the gate and says ...

99 OF MY MATES HAVE BEEN HACKED DOWN, MAYBE I'LL BE LUCKY

No – they wouldn't run into a one-man massacre. The Normans were desperate but not daft. Somebody must have been fibbing.

They may have run from the castle but they would not let themselves be chopped down, one at a time, by an axing earl. Sagas were written about wonderful Waltheof's axe attack. Sagas are poems, telling the story of a great hero. They are a bit long and written in Old English, so here's a new saga written by the *Horrible Histories*' very own captive poet.

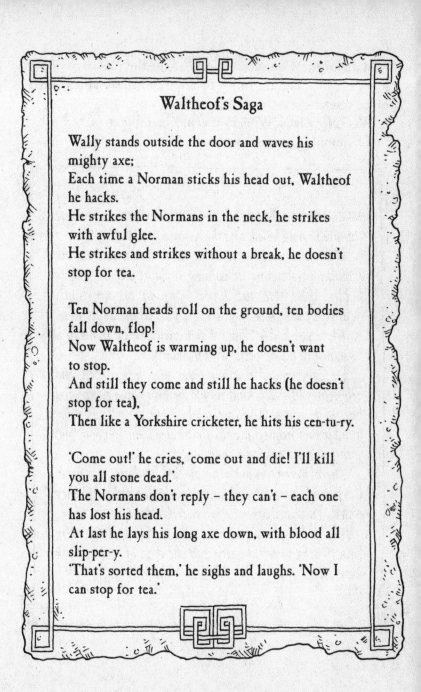

Waltheof's Saga

Wally stands outside the door and waves his
mighty axe;
Each time a Norman sticks his head out, Waltheof
he hacks.
He strikes the Normans in the neck, he strikes
with awful glee.
He strikes and strikes without a break, he doesn't
stop for tea.

Ten Norman heads roll on the ground, ten bodies
fall down, flop!
Now Waltheof is warming up, he doesn't want
to stop.
And still they come and still he hacks (he doesn't
stop for tea),
Then like a Yorkshire cricketer, he hits his cen-tu-ry.

'Come out!' he cries, 'come out and die! I'll kill
you all stone dead.'
The Normans don't reply – they can't – each one
has lost his head.
At last he lays his long axe down, with blood all
slip-per-y.
'That's sorted them,' he sighs and laughs. 'Now I
can stop for tea.'

William the Conqueror heard about the massacre of his men. He marched north for revenge and the Vikings sailed off to safety.

Wise move lads. William was in a bad mood.

The monk, Odericus Vitalis wrote ...

William fell on the English and spared no man. Many were captured, more killed, and the rest put to flight.

William himself went on to comb forests and distant mountains, stopping at nothing to hunt out the enemy hidden there. He cut down many in his vengeance; destroyed the homes of others and burned homes to ashes. Nowhere else had William shown such cruelty. In his fury he punished the innocent with the guilty.

He commanded that all crops and herds, food and belongings of every kind should be brought together and burned to ashes. And so terrible a famine fell upon the humble and helpless people, that more than 100,000 folk, young and old alike, died of hunger.

There weren't enough people left to bury the dead. Corpses of humans and cattle lay in the fields till they rotted. The Northern rebels were crushed.

The Vikings still weren't quite finished. They were back in 1075 to rob the city. But the days of Viking York were over.

Woeful walls

A city needs walls to keep out the nasty neighbours – a bit like you may need a garden fence. The Romans had a wooden fence and a ditch ... feeble. So around AD 210 they put up stone walls. The Saxons didn't do a very good job of looking after them. When the Vikings arrived a writer said ...

The walls were not strong or well built.

New City walls were built between the 1240s and the 1340s – that's what you can see today.

Soldiers guarded the walls and were harshly punished if they fell asleep. How were they punished?

a) They had their eyes put out.

b) They were hung in a basket over the castle moat.

c) They were beaten with nettles.

Answer: **b)** The soldier was given a little food, water and a knife then dangled over the walls. When they'd had enough they could cut the rope, drop into the moat and get a cold bath – and a filthy bath because the castle toilets emptied into the water. They were then banned for a year and a day from the castle.

AWFUL ARCHBISHOPS

York has a huge cathedral known as York Minster. Very pretty.

York Minster is second in the top ten of British cathedrals (at least that's what the Christian church said). It has its own archbishop and you don't get much higher in the church than archbishop ... except God, of course. And God doesn't count because he doesn't go to church.

The bad news for readers of *Horrible Histories* is that most of the Archbishops of York have been pretty boring old blokes. Hardly anything horrible to say about these saintly souls! But here are a few foul facts our dirty detectives have dug up about some bad bishes.

Seeing stars

Gerard was a bit of a troublemaker. He argued with his boss, the Archbishop of Canterbury, and with his boss's boss – the Pope. He wasn't popular with the people of York.

Gerard's crime was to have a book on 'astrology' – that is making horoscopes by looking at the stars.

If YOU want to read your horoscope you just look in a newspaper. But there were no newspapers in 1108 so Gerard had a book that told him how to make up his own horoscopes.

Some people believed this was a 'magic' art. (Well it WOULD be if it worked. Imagine if you could REALLY see into the future. You could pop down to your local shop and get all the numbers right on tomorrow night's lottery!)

One evening Gerard lay down with his 'astrology' book under his pillow. The next morning he was dead.

The monks who found him were horrified...

> AHHH! THE MAGIC BOOK MUST HAVE KILLED HIM!

> DO YOU THINK HE SAW IT COMING?

Gerard had died on his way to a meeting in London and the people of York said, 'Serves you right!'

They also ...
• refused to bury him in the cathedral
• pelted his coffin with stones on its way to the funeral
• said he worked with the Devil to make black magic.[2]

No hope for Scrope

Bad bish Scrope set up a rebellion against King Henry IV. He made a list of all the things he wanted the King to change. He stuck this list up all over York. We don't have a copy. It may have looked like this...

2 York chocolate factories became famous for 'Black Magic' ... selling the chocolates of that name, not selling their souls to the Devil. Did Archbishop Gerard of York give them the idea for the name?

Dear Citizen of York

Please read this.
(If you don't know how to read then get someone to teach you).

I, Richard Scrope, Archbishop of York, want King Henry IV to give us:
• Less tax
• The old royal family back on the throne
• Better government

If he doesn't then we'll rebel. Let's show horrible Henry who counts in this kingdom! Power to the people (and the church, of course).

Richard Scrope

Go! Go! Go with the Battling Bish!

Archbishop Scrope found 9,000 armed men willing to march into battle with him. Then it went a bit wrong. Scrope might have kept a diary about it...

27 May 1405

My army leaves York - on to death or glory -
My God is behind me.

29 May 1405

We meet King Henry's army at Shipton Moor. five
miles north of York. (Yes. I know, five miles in three
days is slower than a sick snail, but my horse is slow-
even though my God is behind him.)

2 June 1405

Our armies have just looked at each other for three
days. I have to say my army looks better than Henry's
but, to be honest I'm not sure an archbishop should be
fighting those rotten, royal bullies. I think it would be best
if I just pack up my tent and march back to York.

3 June 1405 How annoying. I have been arrested and
taken to the king at Pontefract Castle about 30 miles
south of York. I would rather be back in dear old York.

4 June 1405 The good news is I've been taken back 25
miles to my own palace at Bishopthorpe, near York. (My
horse must be getting a bit tired by this time.) The bad news
is I am still under arrest and have been told I must face
a trial for treason. Of course, with my God behind me,
I will be found 'not Guilty'.

8 June 1405 I don't believe it. They have found me
guilty and sentenced me to death. I am to be taken to a
field outside the walls of York, at Skeldergate Postern.
There I will be beheaded. (My horse will probably be glad
of the rest). I must say I think my God has let me down
big time.   End of rebellion.

Archbishop Scrope was beheaded by a man named Thomas Alman. This wasn't a very nice job and no one wanted to do it. But Alman had been a prisoner in York for 15 years. If he axed the Archbishop then he would go free.

Would you hack off a head to get out of jail?

Horrible Histories note: For a *Horrible Histories* reader the answer to this question is 'Of course!'

Alman gave the neck FIVE chops. This was not because he was clumsy – it was because Scrope was a leader of the Christian church in England and Christ had died on the cross with FIVE wounds.

King Henry didn't stay around after the execution but headed north. He didn't get very far before he was struck down by an illness – some said it was leprosy.

He was also haunted by nightmares. He woke up screaming ...

TRAITORS! YOU HAVE THROWN FIRE OVER ME!

The people of York said it was the revenge of the Archbishop!

Spooky Scrope

Archbishop Scrope was forced to ride a bony old horse from Bishopthorpe to his execution in Skeldergate. To make him look really silly he had to face backwards, and he wore a blue cloak with a hood.

Four hundred years later a butcher, Robert Johnson, drove sheep along the same road. He was taking them to be slaughtered and sold in his shop.

It was evening and he was tired. He was angry when the sheep stopped and refused to move. The butcher pushed his way through the frightened sheep to see what was stopping them.

It was a funeral. A coffin was being carried along the road. In front of the coffin was a man in a blue robe. Then Johnson blinked. The coffin was following the man ... but there was no one carrying it! It was drifting along.

The butcher tried to get closer to the coffin and the man but they faded into the evening air.

People of York heard his story. They were sure the butcher had seen the ghostly image of the Bishop on his way to the execution. The coffin would have been carried behind him so his corpse could be taken back to the Minster to be buried. After the creepy coffin vanished the sheep walked on – to their own executions. Robert Johnson refused to go that way ever again.

But why didn't the bony old horse appear in the vision? It's an eerie tail.

Did you know...?
Some people worshipped at the tomb of the dead Archbishop in York Minster. They showed their love by putting tree trunks across his tomb!

Snakes and ladders

Thomas Wolsey started with nothing – like a boy at the start of a game of snakes and ladders. Life for young Thomas was all climbing the ladders to fame and riches. He started as the son of a butcher, but ended up as one of the most powerful men in England.

Of course every life has its snakes as well as its ladders. There were some tricky snakes in Thomas Wolsey's life... And Henry VIII was the slimiest of those snakes.

③ 1514 – The Pope makes Thomas Archbishop of York (because Henry VIII told him to!) – up another ladder.

⑤ Thomas lives at Hampton Court Palace with 400 servants. Can he climb any higher?

④ 1514 – Thomas is now a Cardinal (top assistant to the Pope) AND Chancellor of England (in charge of all the money) – up another two ladders.

② 1509 – He became friends with new young King Henry VIII – up the next ladder.

① 1507 – Thomas became a priest and was given a job by King Henry VII – up that ladder.

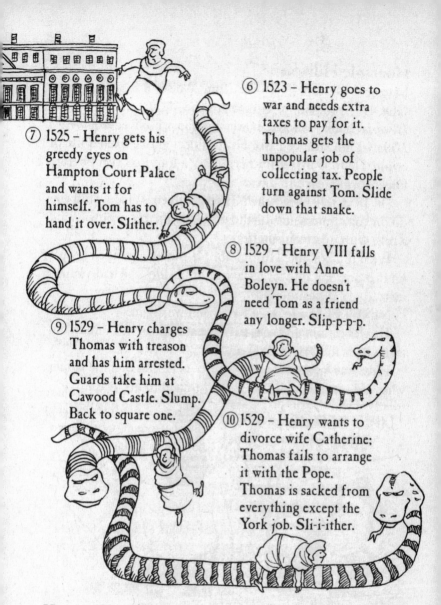

⑥ 1523 – Henry goes to war and needs extra taxes to pay for it. Thomas gets the unpopular job of collecting tax. People turn against Tom. Slide down that snake.

⑦ 1525 – Henry gets his greedy eyes on Hampton Court Palace and wants it for himself. Tom has to hand it over. Slither.

⑧ 1529 – Henry VIII falls in love with Anne Boleyn. He doesn't need Tom as a friend any longer. Slip-p-p-p.

⑨ 1529 – Henry charges Thomas with treason and has him arrested. Guards take him at Cawood Castle. Slump. Back to square one.

⑩ 1529 – Henry wants to divorce wife Catherine; Thomas fails to arrange it with the Pope. Thomas is sacked from everything except the York job. Sli-i-ither.

He set off from Cawood Castle to London and to the Tower for certain execution. But when he got to Leicester, Thomas Wolsey fell ill and DIED!

Henry was cheated of his execution. Thomas kept his head!

Horrible Hutton

Matthew Hutton took over Tom Wolsey's job and was a GOOD Archbishop. So what's he doing in a *Horrible Histories* book, you ask. It was his son who lived a *Horrible Histories* life. Young Luke Hutton decided he liked a life of crime. He took up highway robbery a hundred years before Dick Turpin came to town.

On 18 October 1598, he turned nineteen. What would you do on your nineteenth birthday? Have a party probably and a cake with nineteen candles.

What did horrible Hutton do? He robbed nineteen people on that one day, one for each year of his life – he had victims instead of cake candles.

NINETEEN. He must have been worn out.

He was caught and sent to Newgate Prison in London but taken back to York to be executed.

Luke was hanged for his crimes. As he climbed the ladder what did his father say before he jumped to his death?

LUKE BEFORE YOU LEAP...

Did you know...?
Luke was also a story-teller. He wrote a horrific tale of a ghostly black dog that haunted his London prison...

The book was still popular fifty years after Luke died.

CLIFFORDS TOWER

On a mound in York you can see the ruin of a tower. It's called Clifford's Tower. Because Sir Roger Clifford built it? No ... it could be because Sir Roger Clifford was HANGED in chains there!

The tower was originally a wooden fortress built by the Normans. They called it 'The Great Tower'.

A stone tower was built between 1245 and 1265 because the wooden one burnt down in 1190 ... and killed 150 people who were sheltering there.

It is now called 'Clifford's Tower' after poor old Roger. His crime was to lose the Battle of Boroughbridge against King Edward II in 1322.

But that isn't the most horrible tale of Clifford's Tower.

York has a Viking festival each year. Many years ago it was a custom to have a huge bonfire at Clifford's Tower.

Then someone reminded the people of the 1190 massacre when a different sort of bonfire was made out of Clifford's Tower. The bonfires were stopped. Here's the story behind it...

Murderous massacre

On 16 March 1190 about 150 men, women and children died on that spot. They had been hiding from a mob of York people, out to kill them.

That Friday the mob set fire to the wooden castle that stood on the spot in those days. The trapped men killed their wives and children, then killed themselves. The ones who survived and ran from the flames were grabbed by the manic mob and massacred on the spot.

How can such a thing happen?

Like this ...

IN JULY 1189 – RICHARD I WAS CROWNED IN LONDON. THE RICHEST JEWS IN THE LAND BROUGHT HIM GIFTS – HE SENT THEM AWAY

LEAVE!

A STORY WENT ROUND THAT RICHARD HAD ORDERED THE JEWS TO BE KILLED – A MOB PELTED THE JEWS WITH STONES AND BURNED THEIR HOMES

HEAVE!

A JEW CALLED BENEDICT WAS HURT BUT ESCAPED HOME TO YORK - HE WAS A MONEY-LENDER, KNIGHTS HAD BORROWED MONEY FROM HIM TO GO ON THE CRUSADES

SORE!

BENEDICT BECAME A CHRISTIAN BEFORE HE DIED OF HIS WOUNDS. BUT THE YORK KNIGHTS DIDN'T WANT TO PAY BENEDICT'S FAMILY THE MONEY

POOR!

THE KNIGHTS WENT TO HIS HOUSE, KILLED BENEDICT'S WIFE AND CHILDREN AND STOLE HIS TREASURE. THEY SET FIRE TO HIS HOUSE

ROAR!

How can such a thing happen?

Greed.

Oh, yes, the knights and the mob SAID they wanted to make the Jews become Christians. They SAID they would be doing the Jews a favour.

But they killed Benedict's family so they didn't have to pay back the money they owed. The mob copied them.

They were not Christian warriors – they were murderers and thieves.

For greed.

A Christian also died at the Siege of Clifford's Tower. He was a monk who went to the tower each morning to pray for the defeat of the Jews.

One morning a stone fell from the top of the tower and landed on him. It killed him.

Awful for Aske

In 1536 Robert Aske led a rebellion against Henry VIII. Aske wanted the north to have its own parliament in York.

His army marched from York. Aske called the rebellion a 'Pilgrimage' – a holy journey.

After the York rebels had captured Pontefract Castle crafty Henry VIII said, 'Come to London for a chat and we'll sort everything out.'

Aske fell for it. What happened when he got to London? He was arrested, of course. Henry sent him back to York to die.

Robert Aske was hung in chains from Clifford's Tower. It took him a week to die and his body was left dangling from the tower for a whole year.

TERRIBLE TRUTHS

There are some quirky and quaint facts that are so odd they might just be true. Can you tell the difference? Here are ten 'facts' – just answer 'true' or 'false'.

1 In 1876 William Sharrow of York was chased by one Wooden Leg, shot and scalped. True or false?

2 A Three-legged Mare stood in Knavesmire for 322 years. True or false?

3 In 1862 a railway builder called Harry Higginson found the skeleton of a dodo near York Station. True or false?

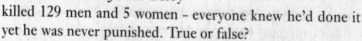

4 Schoolteacher Eugene Aram of York was so famous he had a poem, a play and books written about his life. (That's true.) He was famous for writing horrible history books. True or false?

5 Yorkshire man James Berry killed 129 men and 5 women – everyone knew he'd done it yet he was never punished. True or false?

6 York man George Hudson brought the railways to York. (That's true.) But he didn't enjoy his last rail trip to York. True or false?

7 William Horsfall was shot because he owned a machine called a 'cropper'. (That's true.) A 'cropper' was used to cut ladies' hair. True or false?

8 In the Middle Ages people did not want to go near to lepers. But they allowed lepers to join them in Holy Trinity Church, Goodramgate. True or false?

9 Ivar the Boneless was a Viking ruler of York. (That's true.) In legends the Vikings said Ivar defeated a magic cow. True or false?

10 In 1829 Jonathan Martin was hiding in the cathedral. (That's true.) He spotted a fire and put it out before the mighty Minster burned down. True or false?

Answers:

1 True. William Sharrow went to America and joined the US Army. He became a commander in the troop led by General Custer. In 1876 they made a reckless attack on a war party of Native American Sioux and were massacred. Sharrow was chased by an Indian called Wooden Leg before being shot and scalped.

2 True. The Three-legged Mare was the nickname for the York gallows where criminals were hanged. Edward Hewison was the first man to die there in 1379. Edward Hughes was the last in 1801. The last Three-legged Mare was pulled down in 1812 and became a no-legged mare.

3 False. York man Harry found the bones on the island of Mauritius where the dodos lived. Or do I mean where they died? Anyway, Harry gave the bones to York museum. What happened to Harry? He moved to New Zealand to build railways. He is now extinct.

4 False. He was famous for murdering his friend and hiding the corpse in a cave. Aram owed Daniel Clark a lot of money so in 1745 he killed him – which is cheaper than paying him back, of course. Thirteen years later the skeleton was found and in 1758 Aram was hanged. Terrible teacher and the poem written about him was pretty terrible too. One verse goes...

> *Two sudden blows with a ragged stick,*
> *And one with a heavy stone,*
> *One hurried gash with a hasty knife, –*
> *And then the deed was done:*
> *There was nothing lying at my foot*
> *But lifeless flesh and bone!*

After the murder Aram went off to teach his class!

> *And then I cleansed my bloody hands,*
> *And washed my forehead cool,*
> *And sat among the children young,*
> *That evening in the school.*

What a good lesson: always wash your hands after a murder.

5 True. James Berry was a hangman. His most famous case was the man he DIDN'T hang. In 1885 he had the job of hanging John Lee – Lee had killed his old employer and was sentenced to death. Berry pulled the lever to let Lee drop – but the trapdoor stuck. They tested the thing and it worked. They put Lee back and tried again and failed again. When it failed a third time Lee was spared and sent to prison instead.

GOD WILL NEVER ALLOW ME TO BE EXECUTED

49

The night before the execution Lee had a dream. In the dream he stood on the gallows and the trapdoor failed to open. Weird? Not the weirdest thing.

Oddly, hangman Berry used to have the same dream many times. In the dream he found that he could not hang a man because the trapdoor refused to open. His dream came true. Lee lived 40 years longer than his hangman.

James Berry's other famous victim was Mrs Berry ... no, not his wife but a woman with the same surname. In 1887 he had to hang her for poisoning her daughter. Mr and Mrs Berry actually knew each other, and had danced together at a police ball in Manchester some years before. Her last dance with James Berry was a painful one.

6 True. George didn't enjoy his last trip to York in 1871 because he was dead at the time. He died in London and his coffin was taken home in one of his own trains to York for burial.

The 'Railway King' was carried through York while the Minster bell boomed out a sad goodbye.

PITY THE RAILWAY KING WENT OFF THE RAILS

AND NOW HE'S A SLEEPER!

George was a great man who built over 1,000 miles of railway. He was Lord Mayor of York three times and made York a great railway town.

He was also a bit of a crook – he took money from his railway company to pay for new lines and slipped a lot of it into his own pocket.

His partners found out and he ended up in York prison in 1865.

7 False. A 'cropper' was a machine used in woollen mills to trim the cloth. One worker on the new cropper machine did the work of ten men and women – that meant nine workers were out of a job every time a cropper was used. What did the workers do? They tried to smash the cropper machines to save their jobs. The wreckers were known as 'Luddites'.

Factory owner William Horsfall hated the Luddites. He said...

I will ride through the Luddites' blood till it comes up to my saddle!

That's a lot of blood. But he never got to ride through the red stuff – the Luddites got in first. They shot him dead.

Three Luddites were executed in York for the killing.

You could say they came a cropper ... but you would never see such a bad joke in a *Horrible Histories* book, would you?

8 False. The lepers were forced to sit in a room of their own. They could see and hear the church services through a peephole in their room.

People were afraid of catching leprosy – a disease that makes your skin go blotchy and kills the nerves in parts of your body. In time your fingers and toes can drop off, even an arm or a leg.

Leprosy can be cured now but half a million people in the world still get it every year. And many people still force lepers out of towns.

9 True. The cow was called Sibilja. Some stories said Ivar had weak leg bones so he had to be carried everywhere on a stretcher, but the top half of his body was amazingly powerful. When he met the monstrous and magical Sibilja he fought her with a bow and arrow. His bow was as big as a tree trunk! He shot a huge arrow into each of the cow's eyes.

10 False. Jonathan hid in the Minster so he could set fire to it. He set fire to the choir seats because he had been annoyed by the buzzing of the organ. He left through a window and escaped to Hexham, 100 miles north. The fire was spotted next morning and burned all day. Poor mad Jonathan was caught and locked away.

How was he caught? Because a week before the fire he wrote a letter saying...

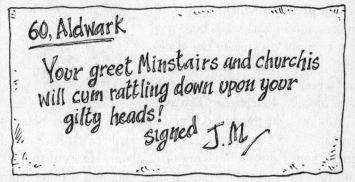

60, Aldwark

Your greet Minstairs and churchis will cum rattling down upon your gilty heads!
signed J.M

Horrible Histories hint: If you want to get away with a crime then DON'T tell people your initials and your address the way Jonathan did.

MICKLEGATE BAR

No this is not a pub – a 'Bar' is a gate in the walls of a city. Micklegate Bar is the south gate of York walls.

It was also the place where traitors' heads were stuck on spikes.

The head boys

In 1460 Richard Duke of York lost the battle of Wakefield (that's 30 miles south of York). His head was stuck up on Micklegate Bar along with the head of his son, Edmund. But a year later Richard's son won the bloody battle of Towton.

Towton was the most bloodthirsty battle ever to take place in England – 35,000 people died. The battle made Richard of York's son, Edward IV, King of England. He went to York and he took down the heads of his father and brother from the city gateway.

In place of his dad's head Ed stuck up the head of their enemy – the Earl of Devon.

Nicking the noddles

Why stick a traitor's head above Micklegate Bar? Two reasons.

1 As a warning to the people of York – 'See what happens if you rebel!'

2 People believed that you had to be buried with your skull and two large bones if you wanted to get into heaven. Taking away the skull meant you never got to heaven and were punished for ever more.

Of course friends tried to pinch the heads and bury them. That was a crime and you could be fined £5.

The Earl of Northumberland was beheaded in Pavement, a street in York in 1572. This was because he was the leader of a rebellion against Queen Elizabeth I.

His head was put on a spike above Micklegate Bar.

One of his friends climbed up and stole the head then buried it at Holy Trinity Church, Goodramgate.

Then someone else dug the head up and returned it to the spike on the city gate.

Last heads

In 1746 there were 22 rebels executed in York – they had been fighting for the Scots at the battle of Culloden and had lost.

The heads were sent around the country but York got to keep two of them – a sort of treat for their part in the executions. The two heads were stuck on Micklegate Bar and were meant to stay there for ever.

But in 1754 they were stolen. A York tailor called William Arundel was fined for stealing the heads.

Arundel also went to prison for two years – a year for each head.

But the heads were never put back and Micklegate Bar has been a head-free zone ever since.

Did you know...?
After the 1746 executions the head of Captain James Hamilton was sent to Carlisle. It was packed in a hatbox! Maybe it was a mistake.

Horrible Histories quick question...
In the 1700s the women of York did not like walking under the arch of Micklegate Bar. Why not?

a) There was a public toilet above the arch and the sewage splashed into the gutter. Their skirts dragged in the pools of poo.

b) It was dark and creepy and they were afraid of being grabbed by the beggars who sheltered there.

c) Heads of traitors were stuck on spikes above the Bar and bits of rotten flesh dropped on people below.

Answer:c) Traitors' heads were left to rot for years and the flesh dropped down into the road. Women complained that it dropped on to them.

SORRY, BUT I DIDN'T DROP ON YOU DELIBERATELY, MADAM

YORK'S FAWKES

One of York's most famous men is Guy Fawkes. Guy was a Catholic, and the Catholics suffered torture, prison and execution when Queen Elizabeth I was on the throne. Then frizzy Lizzie died.

King James I would be better for Fawkes and his friends, wouldn't he?

Er, no. James was just as bad.

The Catholics were desperate. They decided to blow up James and his parliament on 5 November 1605.

Everyone knows the story of how Guy was caught in the cellars. But here are 10 things they don't usually tell you...

1 Guy was born in the Stonegate area of York. He was brought up as a Protestant – not a Catholic. He only became a Catholic in his teens. A deadly decision.

2 Guy was not the leader or the inventor of the Gunpowder Plot. He was brought into the gang because he was a soldier and an expert on gunpowder.

3 Guy was discovered with a ton of gunpowder and arrested just before midnight on 4 November, but he nearly got away with it. On the afternoon of 4 November a search party found Guy with the powder hidden behind piles of firewood. Guy said...

4 Guy was arrested and bravely refused to tell the King's torturers who was in the plot with him. He didn't even tell them his real name. But they searched him and found a letter in his pocket. The envelope said:

5 The King heard that Guy was refusing to talk so he gave an unusual order...

6 When Guy still refused to talk they used more savage torture. Guy Fawkes faced the wicked William Waad at the Tower of London. A Catholic priest called Gerard survived Waad's torture and lived to tell the tale...

Then we went to the place of torture. We went in a sort of solemn procession, attendants going ahead with lighted candles because the place was underground and very dark, especially around the entrance. It was a place of enormous size and in it were all sorts of racks and other instruments of torture. Some of these they displayed to me and told me I should have to taste every one of them. Then again they asked me if I was willing to answer their questions. "It is not in my power", I answered. Throwing myself on my knees I said a prayer or two.

They led me to a great pillar of wood that was one of the supports of this vast crypt. At the top were staples and here they placed my wrists in manacles of iron. They ordered me to mount two or three steps. My arms being fixed above my head, they withdrew those steps one by one so that I hung by my hands and arms.

The tips of my toes, however, still touched the ground since I was so tall. Since they could not raise me higher they dug away the ground beneath me.

Thus hanging by the wrists they asked me if I was willing to confess. I replied, "I neither can nor will." But so terrible the pain was in my breast and belly, my arms and hands. It seemed to me that all the blood in my body had rushed up to my arms and hands.

I was under the impression at the time that the blood actually burst forth from my fingers and at the backs of my hands.

This was, however, a mistake.

Brave Gerard resisted three days of this treatment before he managed to escape from the Tower with the help of a rope. Guy Fawkes was just as brave and held out for several days. But Waad wasn't going to lose a second prisoner down a rope. Guards made sure there would be no escape for Guy Fawkes.

7 Guy and the plotters were executed outside Westminster – the place they had planned to blow up. The execution took place on 30 January 1606.

8 On 5 November 1605 the people of London were ordered to light bonfires and have a party because the King had been saved. In the 1650s the first fireworks were set off with the bonfire parties. In Lewes in Sussex there is a 5 November tradition of setting fire to barrels of tar and rolling them down a hillside. This is extremely dangerous, of course, and the adults find it such hot, thirsty work they have to go to a local pub to drink and cool off. At least that's their excuse!

As a little boy of Lewes wrote in 1822,

The fifth of November's a very good spree;
Special constables all is as drunk as can be.

9 In 1710 boys were first seen begging in the street.

A PENNY TO BURN GUY FAWKES, PLEASE

For many years the people of Scotton village in Yorkshire refused to celebrate 5 November with fireworks and bonfires. This village was where Guy Fawkes had lived and the people didn't think it was fair that Guy should take all the blame.

10 Guy Fawkes went to St Peter's School in York. The school is still there and they have a bonfire on 5 November every year. But they DON'T burn a dummy of Guy the way other bonfire parties do. In the 1940s the school headmaster said...

WE SHOULD NOT BE BURNING OUR OLD PUPILS!

What a sensible school rule. Does your school burn its old pupils? If it does then tell the head teacher to stop at once.

WOEFUL WOMEN

For many men it was tough living in old York. But it could be worse for women.

Here are some sad or savage stories of truly cruel cases. *Horrible Histories* warning: Do NOT read the following if you don't want the gruesome details ...

NAME: ISABEL WARDE

CRIME: BLOCKING THE KING'S SOLDIER'S WAY

DIED: 1539

PUNISHMENT: HACKED TO DEATH

DETAILS:

ISABEL WARDE WAS MOTHER SUPERIOR (THAT MEANS SHE WAS TOP NUN) AT A YORK CONVENT. HENRY VIII DECIDED TO CLOSE ALL THE CONVENTS IN ENGLAND AND SELL THE LAND TO STUFF HIS OWN TREASURE CHESTS. ISABEL STOOD AT THE DOOR AND REFUSED TO LET HENRY'S MEN IN. THEY SENT A TROOP OF SOLDIERS TO DEAL WITH HER. SHE SAID THEY COULD COME IN OVER HER DEAD BODY ... SO THEY HACKED HER DOWN WITH SWORDS AND WENT IN ... OVER HER DEAD BODY.

THE DEAD WOMAN'S HOUSE IS CALLED JACOB'S WELL AND IT STILL STANDS BEHIND HOLY TRINITY CHURCH.

The story COULD be true but some people are not so sure. Still, you can picture the scene, bits of chopped nun scattered over the doorstep.

NAME: MARGARET CLITHEROE
CRIME: REFUSING TO PLEAD GUILTY
DIED: 1586
PUNISHMENT: CRUSHED TO DEATH
DETAILS:

MRS CLITHEROE WAS A CATHOLIC AND REFUSED TO GO TO THE PROTESTANT CHURCH IN YORK AS THE LAW SAID SHE HAD TO. SHE WAS FINED AND WENT TO PRISON THREE TIMES. BUT WHEN SHE WAS CAUGHT HIDING CATHOLIC PRIESTS SHE WAS TAKEN BACK TO COURT AND FACED EXECUTION. THE JUDGES ASKED IF SHE WAS "GUILTY" OR "NOT GUILTY". SHE REFUSED TO SAY "GUILTY" BECAUSE SHE THOUGHT SHE HAD DONE NOTHING WRONG. SHE REFUSED TO SAY "NOT GUILTY" AS THE JUDGES WOULD HAVE FORCED HER CHILDREN TO BETRAY HER. SO SHE WAS SENT TO BE "PRESSED" – CRUSHED UNDER HALF A TON OF STONES. SHE WAS TAKEN TO THE TOLL BOOTH ON OUSE BRIDGE AND STONES WERE HEAPED ON HER TILL SHE DIED. THE JUDGE WAS SUPPOSED TO HAVE SAID...

> *You must return to prison, and there, in the lowest part of the prison, be stripped naked, laid down, your back on the ground, and as much weight laid upon you as you are able to bear, and so to continue for three days without meat or drink, and on the third day to be pressed to death, your hands and feet tied to posts, and a sharp stone under your back.*

In fact Margaret Clitheroe was taken to the Ouse Bridge in the centre of the city. She was not made to suffer three days. A report said...

> They placed the board upon her and the hired executioners placed the huge stones upon her. Within a quarter of an hour she was dead. The sheriffs left the body under the door from nine in the morning until three in the afternoon. They then buried her body in some waste ground, where they hoped it would never be found.

But Margaret's body was found by friends and given a proper burial. We don't know where the body was taken but her hand was removed and is now held at the Bar Convent Christianity museum in York.

A house in The Shambles is open to visitors who want to remember the brave lady.

Did you know...?

Margaret's husband was a butcher and they lived at number 35-6, The Shambles – a street filled with butcher's shops. Sheep and cattle would have been kept behind the shops and slaughtered there. The middle of the street would have been an open gutter. The bloody waste from the butchers would be washed out of the shops and into the street.

Tourists now walk down with cameras. In the Middle Ages they would have needed flippers!

NAME: JENNET PRESTON
CRIME: WITCHCRAFT
DIED: 1672
PUNISHMENT: HANGED
DETAILS:

JENNET WAS A WITCH - OR SO THE PEOPLE OF YORK SAID. SHE WAS BLAMED FOR KILLING A CHILD BUT SET FREE FROM YORK CASTLE. PEOPLE BELIEVED THAT SHE WENT STRAIGHT TO A MEETING WITH OTHER WITCHES AND TOGETHER THEY PLOTTED TO MURDER HER JUDGE WITH MAGIC SPELLS. THE JUDGE WOKE THAT NIGHT, SCREAMING THAT JENNET PRESTON WAS CRUSHING HIM TO DEATH. BY MORNING HE WAS DEAD.

JENNET WAS ARRESTED AND TOLD TO TOUCH THE CORPSE. WHEN SHE DID IT WAS SAID THAT FRESH BLOOD SPURTED OUT OF IT. THAT WAS A SURE SIGN JENNET WAS THE KILLER. SHE WAS HANGED.

HER HUSBAND SAID THAT SHE DESERVED IT.

The 1600s were dangerous times for women who were said to be witches. In York things were not too bad. In 1570 the Archbishop of York, Edmund Grindal, said a witch should be locked away for a year then be made to stand in the pillory.

Often a witch was set free by a judge. Some were told to go to church and say sorry. Some had to pay a fine. Jennet Preston was unlucky and unusual.

Still it could have been worse ...

IN SCOTLAND THEY BURN WITCHES
SO I'M HAPPY TO HANG!

NAME: ELIZABETH BROADINGHAM
CRIME: CONSPIRACY TO MURDER
DIED: 1776
PUNISHMENT: BURNT AT STAKE
DETAILS:
HER HUSBAND JOHN WENT TO PRISON FOR
SMUGGLING AND MRS BROADINGHAM FELL
IN LOVE WITH THOMAS AIKNEY. THEY PLOTTED TO KILL JOHN
IN PRISON BUT FAILED. WHEN HE WAS RELEASED AIKNEY WENT
TO THE HOUSE AND STABBED JOHN IN THE STOMACH.
THE WOUND WAS SO DEEP THE KNIFE WAS LEFT IN THE VICTIM.
THE KNIFE WAS TRACED TO AIKNEY.
HE AND MRS BROADINGHAM WERE ARRESTED AND
SENTENCED TO DEATH. AIKNEY WAS HANGED BUT
MRS BROADINGHAM WAS TIED TO A SLEDGE AND DRAGGED
FROM YORK CASTLE TO THE SCAFFOLD THEY CALLED TYBURN,
WHERE SHE WAS STRANGLED AND HER BODY BURNT AT
THE STAKE – THE PUNISHMENT FOR A WOMAN WHO
KILLED HER HUSBAND. SHE NEVER SHOWED ANY REGRET.

One report says John Broadingham staggered after Aikney shouting, 'Murder! Murder!' Neighbours came to help the stabbed man and found him carrying the knife in one hand. The other hand was holding in his bowels, which were dropping to the ground. He died the next day.

NAME: MARY BATEMAN

CRIME: WITCHCRAFT

DIED: 1809

PUNISHMENT: HANGED

DETAILS:

MARY WAS A BIT OF A CROOK.

SHE SAID SHE HAD MAGIC EGGS - WHEN HER HENS LAID THEM THE WORDS "CHRIST IS COMING" WAS PRINTED ON THE EGGS.

PEOPLE PAID A PENNY A TIME TO LOOK AT THEM.

SHE ALSO COLLECTED MONEY FOR VICTIMS OF A FIRE BUT KEPT IT ALL TO HERSELF.

MARY CLAIMED TO BE A WITCH TOO.

SHE ONCE SAID TO HER HUSBAND...

Her husband hurried off. When he had gone she sold his clothes and all their furniture.

Then Mrs Perigo died and Mary was found guilty of giving her poison. She was hanged in York and her body taken to a hospital where doctors would cut her up for experiments. They charged three pence a time and made £30. They say strips of her skin were sold as lucky charms. Her skeleton is still kept at Leeds University.

Mary was such a crook that she cheated another prisoner out of money in York prison ... even though she knew she was going to be hanged and would never go free to spend it!

NAME: *MOTHER SHIPTON*

DIED: *1561*

DETAILS:

MOTHER SHIPTON SAID SHE COULD SEE INTO THE FUTURE. IN 1530 ARCHBISHOP WOLSEY WAS ON HIS WAY TO YORK.
MOTHER SHIPTON SAID HE WOULD SEE YORK BUT NEVER REACH THE CITY.
THE ANGRY ARCHBISHOP SAID HE'D HAVE HER HANGED AS A WITCH. BUT JUST AS SHE SAID, HE REACHED CAWOOD AND FROM THE TOWER HE LOOKE ACROSS AT YORK, EIGHT MILES AWAY, BUT BEFORE HE COULD LEAVE HE WAS

> ARRESTED BY HENRY VIII'S MEN AND SENT OFF FOR
> EXECUTION. IT IS SAID SHE WAS THE DAUGHTER OF THE
> DEVIL AND THE UGLIEST WOMAN IN THE WORLD.

A book written long AFTER her death (in 1561) gave some of the amazing things she said she could see. The book said Mother Shipton wrote...

The Western King's Wooden Horses
Shall be destroyed by
the Drake's Forces

That was the Spanish Armada attack of 1588: the Spanish King sent galleons ('wooden horses') but were beaten by Sir Francis Drake's English navy. Other things she saw far into her future were the siege of York in 1644 and the Great Fire of London in 1666.

But be warned! She also wrote...

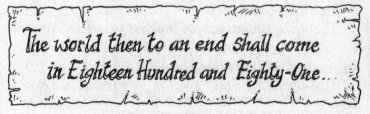

The world then to an end shall come
in Eighteen Hundred and Eighty-One...

See? The world ended in 1881 – you were never born and you are not reading this book because it was never written.[3] How did clever Mother Shipton KNOW that? Amazing.

3 When her book was printed again in 1910 the verse changed to say:
'The world then to an end shall come
In Nineteen Hundred and Ninety-One.'
So you may have been born but you are now dead and are not reading these words. Shame. You have missed reading this brilliant book.

THE TRUTH ABOUT TURPIN

Dick Turpin was a highwayman who was hanged in York. Some people see him as a hero – like Robin Hood, robbing the rich and acting like a gentleman. In fact he was a thug and a bully.

Tales were invented about him and people still believe them. They were lies. Here's his real story...

The keys rattled in the door and the priest walked into the narrow, stinking cell. The prisoner looked up and tried to smile.

'Are you ready to confess, Mr Turpin?' the priest asked. Dick Turpin nodded once. 'I'm sorry for my wicked life – but sorriest of all to be dying in York, so far from home.'

'You were born in Essex, weren't you?' the priest asked.

'Yes. And I was a butcher by trade. But it was so easy to steal cattle and sell the meat – better than paying for the beasts at market. I joined a gang that stole cattle and deer. We made a good living.'

'So what went wrong?'

'The young lad we used as a lookout got scared and told the law. I only just got away,' Turpin said. He took off his light-brown wig and rubbed his head.

'That should have been a lesson – a warning,' the priest said.

'I know but I went and joined another gang. House-breakers. We just armed ourselves with swords and pistols and smashed down someone's door. We robbed them of everything we could carry.'

'That is wicked. But so long as you didn't hurt anyone.'

Turpin sighed. 'I didn't say that. There was one farmer wouldn't tell us where his money was hidden. We pulled down his trousers and roasted his backside over his fire. I can still remember the smell of him burning.'

'And the highway robbery?'

'Ah, that was easy. We stopped travellers and threatened to shoot them if they didn't hand over their money,' Turpin shrugged.

'At least you didn't murder anyone,' the priest said and patted Turpin's knee.

'I didn't say that,' Turpin said again and spread his hands. 'A gamekeeper caught me poaching in Epping Forest. I shot him.'

The priest looked up to the damp ceiling. 'May God forgive you,' he muttered.

'I ran off to Yorkshire where no one knew me.

'But you didn't give up your life of crime, did you?'

'No. I stole horses - that's why they locked me in York Castle.' He thumped the wooden bench he was sitting on. 'I'd have got away with that too but I shot a cockerel. I was caught for shooting a cockerel! How stupid. Maybe I deserve to die for being so stupid.'

'They arrested you for shooting the cockerel ... then realized you were a horse thief.'

Turpin nodded. 'But they still didn't know I was the man they wanted for the Epping Forest murder. I was betrayed by a letter. I wrote to my brother and asked for his help. Then I had the Devil's own bad luck,' he groaned.

'Maybe it wasn't the Devil's luck. Maybe it was God's way of stopping you,' the priest frowned.

The prisoner shrugged. 'Whatever. My old schoolmaster saw the letter in the post office. He knew my handwriting and knew I was wanted for murder. You know the rest.'

'You were put on trial and found guilty.'

'And I hang this morning,' Turpin said.

There were footsteps in the corridor and the door swung open. A man in a black hood said, 'It's time.' He bound the prisoner's hands behind his back and led him roughly out of the cell and the castle.

Turpin climbed wearily on to a horse-drawn cart and was carried through the gateway of the castle and along Castlegate.

Crowds lined the route as he made his way over Ouse Bridge, along Ousegate and up the steep slope of Micklegate. The cart passed through Micklegate Bar, on to Blossom Street, The Mount, and finally the Knavesmire.

An even larger crowd had gathered here. 'I have sinned,' Turpin cried to the mob but his voice creaked. 'I deserve my fate!' The executioner slipped the rope around the horse thief's neck and Turpin turned to the priest.

'May God forgive me,' he said softly.

'May God forgive you,' the priest echoed.

He climbed the ladder and the rope was fastened tightly to the gallows. Turpin threw himself off the ladder boldly and the crowd roared. He was dead within a few minutes.

Ten truths about Turpin ...

1 Dick Turpin never owned a horse called Black Bess. If you think he did you are probably a black pudding.

2 Turpin never made the famous ride from London to York – that was a tale told about another road robber, John Nevison. A writer simply pinched the Nevison story and tacked it on to the Turpin tale.

3 Turpin was not a handsome hero. His face was covered with smallpox scars.

4 He wasn't hanged for highway robbery – he was hanged as a horse thief. But he really was caught for stupidly shooting a cockerel. Cock-a-doodle-boom.

5 He had a partner called Matthew King. In most stories King is called 'Tom' King by mistake. It was said that Turpin met King when he tried to rob him on a forest trail. Instead of robbing him the two villains joined forces. This story is almost certainly another lie.

6 It is probably true that Turpin shot King by accident. He was aiming to shoot the man who had arrested King but killed his friend instead. King died with some famously daft last words.

Dick, you have killed me.

But was Turpin really such a rotten shot? Or did he shoot King to silence him?

7 Turpin stole horses in the north and sold them in the south of England. The man who helped him sell the stolen horses was his own dad. Dad was arrested but never hanged. Shame. He could have kept his son company and swung together – Dad and lad, side by side.

8 Turpin had a wife - a serving girl called Elizabeth. She was arrested for helping Turpin with his robberies but released. She DID help Turpin to hide and looked after him when he was forced to shelter in a cave.

9 Turpin's body was then taken back to the centre of York and kept in the Blue Boar Inn in Castlegate overnight. In those days a public house often had a room that was used to store bodies! Nice pub grub.

10 His body was buried THREE times. First near St George's Church in York, but it was dug up, maybe by doctors who wanted to cut it up for experiments. Then it was buried in a doctor's garden. Turpin's friends stole it back. Finally he was buried in quicklime – that turned the corpse to mush, so doctors couldn't carve it up. His gravestone can still be seen in St George's Churchyard.

Grim gallows

You can go to York today and feel safe from hanging. But you may not be safe from the miserable memories of the sad scenes that happened at the horrible hangings. Cheer up the tourists by telling them these horrid happenings.

Did you know...?

...the gallows in Knavesmire where Dick Turpin died are gone There's a race-course there now.

HORSES WIN BY A NECK WHERE CRIMINALS LOST BY A NECK!

...until 1700 the Archbishops of York had their own gallows in Fossgate and other spots round the city.

THE YORK CHURCH HAD MORE PEOPLE
HANGED THAN THE LAW DID!

…there's a street called Thief Lane in York. It's the lane
crooks were taken down to their executions.

ON THE JOURNEY BACK THEY
PROBABLY CALLED IT DEAD
THIEF LANE

…there were gallows on the main road into York. But it was
a nasty way to greet visitors. They were taken down in 1801
and moved nearer the castle.

SO THE CASTLE WAS THE
DEAD CENTRE OF THE CITY!

…the castle gallows was given a cheerful name.

 THEY WERE CALLED THE NEW DROP

…the Windmill pub was close to the New Drop. It was
packed on Friday afternoons – execution day.

YOU COULD ENJOY A NICE DROP
AT THE NEW DROP

…the law stopped hanging in public in 1868. The executions
moved inside the castle.

THE CRIMINALS COULD DIE
IN PEACE. THAT'S NICE!

...the last hanging inside the castle took place in 1896. Murderer August Carlsen was hanged.

ODDLY ENOUGH IT WAS AUGUST CARLSEN'S LAST HANGING TOO!

AMAZING! WAIT TILL I TELL THE FOLKS BACK HOME

York talk

If you are going to visit York then you need to know some of the old English words they still use in the area. Here are a phairly phoul phourteen phrases – how many can you guess? Clue: it's not a very nice story...

ONE **DOWLY** DAY ME FRIEND GAVE ME A **CROGGY** SO WE COULD TAKE A **GANDER** AT THE **FELL** WITH OUR **BAGGINS**. BUT I ATE TOO MANY **SPOGGS** AND THE RIDE MADE ME **CHUCK ME GUTS UP** IN THE **CLUDGER**... IT **GOFFED** LIKE A **MIDDEN**. I GOT ME **KEGS** DIRTY AND I **HAD A RIGHT MONK ON**. ME MA GAVE US A **BAZZERKIN**.

Answers:
One misty day me friend gave me a ride on a bicycle crossbar so we could take a look at the moor with our packed lunch. But I ate too many sweets and the ride made me be sick in the toilet – it stank like a rubbish heap. I got me trousers dirty and I was in a bad mood. Me Ma gave us a telling off.
Well? How did you score? Get twelve and you are a genius. Get FOURTEEN and you are a rotten cheat because there are only thirteen phrases.

CITY OF SPOOKS

York is an ancient place and lots of people have died there. Some have died there horribly. So it is not surprising that the city has its share of spooks. If you are scared of ghosts then read about these with your eyes closed…

All Saints Church

Thirty-nine Mayors of York are buried here. (Why are they buried at All Saints? Because they are dead.)

I was at All Saints Church for a funeral when a beautiful young woman in white drifted through the church. They say she's the spirit of a poor girl who died but never had a proper burial. Now she haunts funerals looking for her own resting place.

The Old Black Swan Inn, Coney Street

The Inn has been knocked down but the ghost still hangs around.

Old Nance died here. She fell in love with a highwayman but he threw her out into the cold when he was tired of her. An old boyfriend, Tom the coach driver, saw her by the side of the road near a village called Sheriff Hutton, just north of York. He picked her up and raced to the Black Swan Inn to get her warmed and fed. Too late. She died that night but had promised that her ghost would protect Tom's family when they were in danger. She kept her word!

Good Old Nance still appears by the roadside on foggy nights to warn drivers on the A64 of danger ahead.

Stockton on the Forest
This village is a couple of miles to the north-east of York city.

> Back in 1812 I was a shepherd at Stockton on the Forest. One night I saw an army march up the hill dressed in white. Their leader was dressed in red. Suddenly an army in dark uniforms appeared and started a battle. The smoke from the cannon covered the hill. When it cleared the armies had vanished.

The sheep must have been flocking to see that.

Holy Trinity Church
This church is on the south side of Micklegate in York city. It was built around 1089.

> The plague came to York many times. They say a father died of plague and was buried in Holy Trinity Church. But when his child died of plague a new law said victims had to be buried outside the city walls. His wife died of a broken heart and was buried next to her husband. I've seen her restless ghost wander through the graveyard looking for her lost child. Sometimes she meets the child and hugs it, but is forced to walk back to her grave, weeping and waving goodbye.

Goodramgate

This lane beside Holy Trinity Church was host to a ghost from the 1500s.

Thomas Percy, Earl of Northumberland, tried to rebel against Queen Elizabeth I in 1572. He ran away to Scotland but was dragged back in chains to York. He was beheaded and his head stuck on a spike at Micklegate Bar. It stayed there for years till it was rescued by friends and buried near Goodramgate. That's where I've seen him wandering among the graves with his head tucked under his arm.

Other spook spotters have said he ambles through The Shambles on quiet nights. (Maybe when the graveyard's too full of brambles for rambles.)

King's Manor

This medieval manor house was used by the Tudor and Stuart royal families.

Henry VIII's wife, Catherine Howard, came here with Henry in 1541. But she started flirting with a man called Thomas. Henry found out and was furious. He had them both executed. I have seen her walk out from a cupboard and walk straight through me. She was wearing a green dress and carrying an armful of roses. Poor young woman.

Henry called Cath his 'Rose without a Thorn'. But in the end nothing was very rosy in her world.

Marston Moor
This moor is outside York. The armies of Charles I marched out to battle from York – but only the ghosts of the dead marched back...

In 1932 I was driving round York looking for the Wetherby road when I saw a group of ragged men wandering by the side of the road. As I got nearer I saw they were dressed in the clothes from the days of King Charles I. They didn't seem to hear me when I asked if they were all right. They didn't even see the bus that came along and drove over them. But when the bus had passed there was no sign of the men. I had seen a troop of ghosts.

The ghosts were probably the spirits of the Cavalier soldiers who fought at Marston Moor in 1644. The King's men were beaten and would have travelled that road as they fled back into York. Where was that bus when they needed it for their getaway?

St William's College
This college was built in 1461 near the Minster. It was named after William the Conqueror's great-grandson, William Fitzherbert.

I won't go near St William's College at night. Two brothers lived here in 1550. One night a rich priest walked by and the brothers slit his throat and stole his purse. The younger brother was terrified by the crime. The older brother was worried he'd go to the law so he went himself and told them the younger brother had done it. The younger brother was hanged and never knew who had given him away. It is the guilty older brother who walks the St William's College pathways, moaning.

You may still hear moaning from this priests' college today. Don't worry. It's probably some student just got his exam results.

The Theatre Royal

This theatre is over 250 years old so it has seen a lot of drama in its painful past.

I was an actress at the Theatre Royal in the 1930s. One evening I saw the ghostly figure of a nun in grey. She vanished into thin air. It seems there was a convent on this spot. The young nun fell in love with a man and was punished horribly by the other nuns. They shut her up in a room with no windows, Then they bricked up the door. What a dramatic way to die!

York Minster

York had an important church right from the days of the Romans. The Normans built a bigger stone cathedral. But the sacred skyscraper you see today, York Minster, was started around 1220 and was finished in no time at all ... well, 250 years. It's seen its share of spooky spirits...

I loved my brother dearly. One day we agreed that if one of us died we'd come back and tell the other. He then went off to join the Navy. I was in York Minster one evening when I saw him walk towards me. He whispered in my ear, "There is a life after death." Then he walked away. I knew he could not be there in the Minster. I knew he must have died and come back to tell me, just as we agreed. Sure enough, a week later, I heard that he had been killed. His ghost told me first.

A chilling chapter in the church's history.

WHAT DO YOU KNOW ABOUT YORK?

Time to turn the tables on your teacher. Ask them these simple questions about the horrible history of York. See how horrible your teacher really is. If they score more than eight then they are so horrible they could have got a job in York Castle torturing people! If you can't find a teacher to torment then see how you score yourself.

> *Horrible Histories* note: Cheating is allowed.

1 In 927 the Viking Turfrid was defeated at York and ran away. He then had an accident and became food for what?

a) fish

b) rats

c) tortoises

HE COULD DO WITH SOME LETTUCE

2 In 1076 the York rebel, Earl Waltheof, was saying the Lord's Prayer while he waited to be executed. He said, 'Lead us not into temptation,' then his head was struck off. What happened next?

a) The head bounced on the ground and hit the executioner in the face.

b) The head hit the ground and finished the prayer.

c) A bolt of lightning frizzled the executioner. (God was a bit upset that the prayer was cut short.)

SHOCKING!

3 In the 1200s a woman from Murton near York fell sick.

What did she blame?
a) Her friend poisoned her
Yorkshire pudding.
b) A frog, baked in her bread
c) Her husband cast a spell
on her.

4 A 1600s house in York is known as 'The Plague House'.
Why?
a) Because the house was covered in mysterious purple spots
like someone with the plague.
b) Because someone in the house had the plague.
c) Because someone in the house didn't have the plague.

5 In the 1700s a gravedigger returned to a York churchyard
and dug up the coffin he had buried that afternoon. Why?
a) He'd lost his false teeth and thought he might have buried
them with the coffin.
b) He'd lost his glasses and mistook the grave for a new one.
c) He was planning to rob the corpse.

6 A 1700s tough teacher from near York punished a boy. The
teacher broke what?
a) three canes across the boy's backside
b) three of the boy's teeth
c) three of the boy's cricket bats

7 In 1786 the first one appeared on
the streets of York. First what?
a) road sweeper
b) traffic warden
c) fast-food stall

8 In York in the early 1800s Mutton Curry killed 117 people. How?

a) Mutton Curry was served in a filthy restaurant and gave customers food poisoning.

b) Mutton Curry was York slang for terror. ('Mutton Curry' = worry.) Mutton curry was a sheep disease that humans could catch at the market. You felt sick and your wool fell out.

c) Mutton Curry could put a rope round your neck and hang you.

9 In 1832 John Barnes got a Christmas parcel that killed him. What was it?

a) an exploding Christmas pudding from a neighbour who hated him

b) a box of his dead sister's clothes

c) a Christmas turkey that he cooked and ate but choked on a bone

10 In the 1850s the rich people of York had sewers to send their toilet waste into the river. (Fancy a swim?) The poor people just had buckets that were emptied on to a cart every night. But what happened to the poo then?

a) It was tipped into the river along with the rich folk's sewage.

b) It was fed to hens so they could lay better eggs.

c) It was spread over the fields so they could give richer corn.

Answers:

1a) A writer of the time said...

> *Not long after he fled from York, Turfrid was shut up in a castle. He slipped past his guards and escaped. Turfrid, losing his life quickly after by shipwreck, became a food to fishes.*

2b) The execution took place on 31 May 1076. After giving away his clothes to the poor, Waltheof spent his last moments in prayer. The executioner was bored – he thought Waltheof was taking too long. He drew his sword and struck just as Waltheof got to: 'Lead us not into temptation.' The head was heard to say, in a clear voice, 'But deliver us from evil. Amen.'

3b) The woman lived in Murton on the edge of York. She said she ate a frog baked in bread. We don't know why she did this and she is too dead to ask. But we do know how to cure it. She prayed to St William of York to cure her and he did.

You may like to try praying to Saint Billy if you swallow a frog ... or if your family car is in a crash...

PLEASE, SAINT WILLIAM OF YORK, HELP OUR CAR. IT'S BEEN TOAD AWAY!

4c) The house in Minster Yard is known as 'The Plague House'. The people of York were terrified when the Great Plague of 1665 came to the city. When a little girl fell sick they were sure she had the plague. Instead of nursing her they locked her up in the house so no one else would catch it. They left her without food and water so after a few dreadful days she died.

She didn't have the plague. You could say the people of York murdered her. That's why her pale, tear-streaked face can be seen at the window. Go and see for yourself. Hear her sad cries...

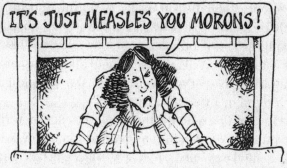

5c) In those days they used to bury people with their jewellery. The gravedigger knew that some valuable rings had been buried with this corpse and he was keen to have them. The funeral was held and he lowered her into the grave. While her friends said prayers he covered the coffin lightly with soil. That evening, when it was quiet, he returned, forced the lid from the coffin, and began to cut the rings from the fingers.

But he clumsily cut the fingers of the lady in the coffin. The lady was not dead, but had been buried in a coma.

The pain in her fingers woke her and she sat up. The gravedigger was terrified. She recovered and went home.

6b) Teacher John Walker was a vicious man. One pupil had three teeth broken when wild Walker punched and kicked him.

Of course Mr Walker didn't spend all his time beating up pupils. He had other punishments too. He would...
• put a pupil in a wooden chest and close the lid
• stand a pupil on a high window-sill
• lie a pupil on a cold church floor
• make a pupil wear all the hats of his class piled on his head.
But smashing the teeth was probably his nastiest.

7a) The man was called a 'scavenger' but he didn't just have to sweep up the rubbish. He had to collect all the animal poo that was dropped in the streets. Nice job. Fancy it?

8c) William Curry was a sheep-stealer so he was known as 'Mutton' Curry. He was sentenced to hang twice...

No, no! He was sentenced twice to hang, I meant. He was let off both times. Then he was sentenced to be sent to prison in Australia. While he was waiting for the next boat to the prison colony the jail offered him a job as York's hangman. Mutton was happy to take the job and did it for 33 years.

On his first attempt he was too drunk to get the rope round the victim's neck. The crowd were angry and cried out...

At last he got the rope round his victim's neck and pulled the lever to open the trapdoor.

The victim fell through ... and so did Mutton Curry!

9b) John Barnes's sister died in Leeds on 11 December 1832. She was buried and her clothes were packed off to her brother who lived near York. But she had died of cholera. The clothes carried the disease to John. By Boxing Day he had stomach pain and diarrhoea. On 29 December he was dead.

Now the GOOD news! York doctor John Snow studied the case. He worked out how cholera was spread so has helped save millions of lives since then.

John Barnes died so others could live!

Snow's discovery was too late to save the people who died in the cholera epidemic of 1832. Between York railway station and the city wall there is a piece of ground with some gravestones. This was the burial place of the cholera victims. 187 people died.

10c) The fields smelled a bit, of course, but the farmers paid well for this muck. The wheat grew and made nice bread which you ate and then went to the toilet which was tipped on the cart and spread on the fields which meant the wheat grew and made nice bread ... get the idea?

BRUTAL BEDERN HALL

We all know history teachers do terrible things – they take poor pupils on school trips to York and don't tell them the horrible bits, just give them boring worksheets to scribble on in the rain.

But, believe it or not, there were even WORSE teachers in York's putrid past! Look at Bedern Hall – a 1300s building in the centre of York.

In the 1800s the area round the old Bedern chapel was full of slums. The city wanted to get the poor children off the streets, so in 1873 they set up a school for them at Bedern Hall – The Bedern National School, known as 'The Ragged School'.

They gave the teaching job to Mr Pimm and told him the more pupils he took in the more money he would be paid.

He became a sort of city child-catcher.

He also had a terrible tale to tell. If you don't believe me, just ask him!

YOU HAD TO FEED AND CLOTHE THE CHILDREN?  BUT I STARVED THEM AND LET THEM DRESS IN RAGS. I KEPT THE MONEY FOR MYSELF!

 BUT THAT WOULD KILL THEM!  A LOT DIED, OF COURSE, BUT I STILL COLLECTED THE MONEY FOR THEM

WHAT ABOUT THE COST OF THE FUNERALS?  FUNERALS? I STUFFED THEM IN A CUPBOARD

BUT THEY WOULD ROT AND SMELL  WHEN THE BODIES ROTTED I BURIED THEM IN SHALLOW GRAVES

AND YOU GOT AWAY WITH IT?  OF COURSE, UNTIL THE BRATS STARTED SCREAMING!

THE RAGGED CHILDREN SCREAMED? NO! THE DEAD ONES! I COULD HEAR THEM SCREAM IN THE CUPBOARD!

Some reports say he was hanged.

The school closed. It was a pork pie factory until 1971. People say that the restless spirits of the dead children are still seen, or heard, near Bedern Hall. Stop and listen to their playful laughter, but the laughter soon changes into screams of terror.

Sometimes they say you feel the cold hand of a child clinging to yours.

Did you know...?
You can get married in Bedern Hall these days. But if you do, you may hear the happy laughter of bridesmaids and page boys.

EPILOGUE

This book can tell you the horrible history of York. But really you need to go there and see the place for yourself. Lots of trains go there (thanks to George Hudson).

Enjoy your visit and don't worry about the putrid past.

Don't worry about being hanged at Knavesmire and having your head stuck on Micklegate Bar ... even if you DO end up executed it won't hurt as much as Archbishop Scrope's five chops.

Don't worry about being robbed by Dick Turpin ... he's dead, and now the only highway robbers are the traffic wardens who make you pay to park.

And don't even worry about having your lungs ripped out by Vikings, being crushed to death by the pressing torture or sent up in flames by Fawkes.

Those grim old days are long gone. Only the lonely ghosts remain. They will probably watch you walking down the narrow streets but you won't be afraid, will you? No!

Don't worry about getting got by the ghosts of old York ... they will probably be more frightened by a *Horrible Histories* reader than you will be of them.

If you don't believe me then go and look in a mirror.